HOLLY AND IVAN'S CHRISTMAS ADVENTURE

Oliver Lansley

HOLLY AND IVAN'S CHRISTMAS ADVENTURE

Inspired by an original idea by Pins and Needles Productions

With illustrations by Zoe Squire

OBERON BOOKS
LONDON

WWW.OBERONBOOKS.COM

First published in 2011 by Oberon Books Ltd
521 Caledonian Road, London N7 9RH
Tel: +44 (0) 20 7607 3637 / Fax: +44 (0) 20 7607 3629
e-mail: info@oberonbooks.com
www.oberonbooks.com

A catalogue record for this book is available from the British
Library.

ISBN: 978-1-84943-136-1

Cover design by Zoe Squire

Contents

For Archie, Poppy and Charlie

Foreword by Oliver Lansley

I have not written exclusively for the demographic of under 6 year olds before and whilst finding it rather daunting have also found it extremely liberating.

With children you don't face any of the usual preconceptions you get from a theatre audience, there's no snobbery, or inverted snobbery, there's no social or political agenda, there are no tastes or opinions or preconceived notions of what is a 'good' or 'important' piece of theatre – all they care about is if they like it or not, or indeed if they are prepared to sit their bums still, and keep their mouths closed for the ensuing 50 minutes of the production. If you don't keep them engaged, it's all over – they won't sit politely and mutter their derision over a glass of chardonnay in the interval – they will let you know, there and then.

This for me is a wonderful challenge and what theatre is all about. You have to continually work and offer your audience new thoughts and new ideas, you have to engage them visually and aurally and you truly have to capture their imaginations.

I still remember vividly my first experiences of theatre and it is really thrilling to think that we might be providing youngsters with that same experience. An experience that can shape their imaginations for years to come.

The other thing I like about writing for children is they are still at a stage where they love language and find it continually fun and fascinating – As do I.

As we grow up people seem to treat language in a much more perfunctory manner, we stop revelling in the way words sound as they roll around our mouths, the silly noises they make, the rhymes, the alliteration and onomatopoeia and so it was very exciting to be able to indulge this passion of mine.

It may sound obvious but work like this is written to be read aloud and in this text we have elected to publish the 'bedtime story' version alongside the scripted version. I hope this will encourage parents and even children themselves to read, remember and re-enact this story as much as they wish.

Finally, when discussing story ideas with Em and Zoe, *Holly and Ivan* immediately jumped out at me as something I wanted to write for two main reasons; my niece and nephew... Archie and Poppy.

And so this is my Christmas present to them (and of course their older brother Charlie). Merry Christmas and I hope Holly and Ivan make it to your stocking in time for Christmas day.

Introduction by Emma Earle

Holly and Ivan's Christmas Adventure is a magical quest story about twins who find themselves lost in the snow on Christmas Eve after falling off Santa's sleigh. We join Holly and Ivan as they journey through a variety of evocative worlds and encounter a range of colourful characters, before arriving at their new owners' home on Christmas morning.

I'm one of those people who really love Christmas so I was thrilled when Pins and Needles (the theatre company I run with Zoe Squire) was invited to work with the Lyric Hammersmith on this production. Once Zoe and I had come up with the idea for the story, we approached Oliver Lansley to write it. We've worked with Oli on a number of other projects and knew that his passion for Roald Dahl and Dr Seuss combined with his love of the English language would result in a piece of writing that would lend itself brilliantly to the stage; rich with words, imagery, textures and Christmassy jollity.

In adapting Oli's short story, the company spent four days workshopping the piece at the Lyric, experimenting with possible theatrical approaches and ways of dividing up the narration between three performers (no mean feat given that there are seventeen characters that speak plus the potential for countless non-speaking roles). We looked at how music might be incorporated into the piece, how we could use puppets, and, crucially, what world the storytellers were from.

Before rehearsals began, Oli and I worked closely together to develop the script: tightening the structure, tweaking a rhyming couplet here or there, and focusing on the clarity of the story. In parallel I worked with the composer Tom Elstob and the designer Zoe Squire on creating a visual and aural identity for the piece that felt magical, Christmassy and warm. We looked at a host of different influences, from music boxes and snow globes, to patchwork quilts and Japanese gardens.

Working on an original story that is set in a timeless, fantasy landscape is an immensely freeing experience. It's invigorating to take the notion of an underwater world and look at how this might be realised. We researched Esther Williams, Busby Berkeley and endless nature documentaries before attempting to translate some of the feelings and impressions these references had left us with into a physical expression on stage. When envisioning the jungle world, we pictured Rio Carnival mixed with elements of Vegas or the Paris Lido. For the desert world, we saw Motown Camel Triplets dancing under a starry mirror ball, set against the backdrop of a giant follow-spot shaped moon.

For me, this production was an attempt to convey the pleasing warm feeling that I experienced reading Oli's story for the first time. We wanted to make something that would engage the imaginations of children aged 2-6 but that would also charm their families. To do this, we used a variety of different theatrical techniques including puppetry, live music and dance, and we approached all of the above with enthusiasm and a willingness to make fools out of ourselves. We wanted to celebrate the joy to be had from dancing wildly, playing with a toy doll, or singing out of key, as well as the more traditional skills of storytelling. I believe you're never too old for Christmas and that a seasonal show is a special event, one that should be savoured by the actors as they share their story with new faces each performance.

THE STORY

Holly and Ivan were two little twins,
They wore the same clothes and they said the same things.
But Holly and Ivan were different from most,
Which probably sounds like a ridiculous boast.
As each boy and girl is unique, in their own special way.

Like Sarah Spondel from Scagglethorpe shall we say...
Whose nose curves up so much at the end
That skiers might wish to jump from the bend.

Or Billy Birthwhistle from Bognor who's quite a strange sight,
As his left ear is a good deal smaller than his right.
Which makes it look slightly further away,
Making Billy appear to always face the wrong way.

But Holly and Ivan differed from most girls and boys.
Because Holly and Ivan were actually... Toys!
Rag dolls to be precise, with button eyes and woollen hair,
Stitched up and sewn with a great deal of care.

They were born in Santa's grotto far far far away,
Where it's so cold, that sometimes even the words that you say
Will freeze the instant they're spoken aloud,
Meaning sentences as well as snow need to get ploughed.

They were made by elves, a peculiar race,
Who are pointy of ear, and rosy of face!
Now Elves don't receive money for the toys that they make,
Instead they are given their payment in cake.
Fairy cakes to be precise as they don't eat much else,
Which to be honest I'm not sure is good for their health.

Bacon fairy cakes for breakfast, or fried egg ones for brunch,
Then cheese and cucumber fairy cakes will follow for lunch.
And some sausage and chips fairy cakes for supper and tea,
With a nice fairy cake for pudding, if they're still hungry.

* * *

Now our story starts on that one special night,
That fills every new toy with a sense of delight.
Monday? I hear one Simple Simon suggest...
No not Monday, you fool, Mondays aren't the best.
Easter perhaps? Or Bonfire night?
Well they're both indeed fun but they're still not right.

It's Christmas Eve of course! That one day of the year,
That fills every new toy with a sense of good cheer.
Because it's the day that they meet their new families.
All those little boys and girls who've been doing good deeds.
Like helping old ladies to put on their hats,
And knitting woollen jackets for bald dogs and cats.

And so we begin on that bestest of days,
With Santa starting to fill up his sleigh.
The toys jostled for a place at the front of the queue.
'Don't worry,' Said Santa, *'There's room for all of you...*
Then he pulled open his sack and said, *'In you go...'*
And followed this up with a mighty, *'Ho Ho Ho...'*

Santa had a strange habit of ho ho ho-ing when he spoke,
Even if what he'd said wasn't really a joke.
Now it was usually fine, him being always amused,
But it became a bit awkward if he was given bad news.

'I'm sorry to hear your frog died ho ho ho…
What do you mean I sound happy?
I'm sad don't you know ho ho ho ho ho ho ho ho…'

As the queue of toys started to jump in the sack,
Poor Holly and Ivan were stuck at the back.
And soon the sack was so full, right up to the brim,
That Holly and Ivan almost didn't fit in.
But before they could speak up Santa shouted,
'Go! Ho ho…' And the reindeers reared up
 and sped off through the snow.

Holly and Ivan held on as tight as they could,
But as the sleigh's speed got faster it was simply no good,
Their raggy doll fingers just couldn't hold on,
And with a big gust of wind, that was it, they were gone.

They tumbled through the air to the earth far below,
And were lucky to land in a big pile of snow.
'Where are we?' Moaned Holly, as she rubbed her bruised bum.
'I must say that falling really isn't much fun.'

Ivan got to his feet and looked all around,
Suddenly feeling much more lost than found.
'I think that we're nowhere, and this is the middle,
But what we do next? Well that's really a riddle.'

Then suddenly they spotted, a most peculiar thing,
Two tags of brown paper, both tied on with string.
And on each tag were names, of a young girl and boy,
'They must be our owners!' Squealed Holly with joy.

'Archie and Poppy,' Read Ivan with care,
'Well I must say they sound like a most pleasant pair'.
'We must find them!' Said Holly, *'Whatever it takes!*
They can't wake up without presents, for Christmas sakes!'

But how will they find them? And where will they go?
And when will they get there, I simply must know!
Can they really succeed in their Christmassy quest?
Well if you stop asking questions then I'll tell you the rest…

* * *

The pair walked for hours through the freezing cold snow,
Neither of them knowing which way they should go.
They shivered with cold as the wind rushed around,
And fresh snowflakes fell fast and covered the ground.

Until finally through the blizzard a furry figure drew near…
'It's the abominable snowman!' Cried Ivan in fear.
Then he hid behind Holly, but out of the snow,
Instead of a monster came a smiley Eskimo…

'I knew it wasn't a monster' Said Holly, shaking her head,
'So did I…' Replied Ivan, though his face went quite red.
'So sorry to trouble you, but are you Archie or Poppy?'
The Eskimo looked down at this strange talking dolly.
'I'm Sorry,' He said,
'I don't know who they are…'
Then leaned in with a smile and did something bizarre.

He bent down and rubbed his red nose against theirs,
Poor Holly was really caught quite unawares.
'Don't worry,' Whispered Ivan, *'That's how they say Hi'*
But she was too busy blushing to give a reply.

'So lovely to meet you' The Eskimo cried,
'We're about to have dinner, so come on inside!'

Then through the snowfall they spotted a light,
And a house built of ice cubes emerged from the night.

'It's an igloo!' Cried Ivan,
'An ig-who?' Replied Holly
'It looks like a super-sized tortoise ice lolly!'

'Don't be so silly, there's people inside.'
Ivan said with a sigh and a roll of his eyes.
And poking out from the roof they could clearly see,
The top of a colourful Christmas tree!

* * *

And so in they walked to the big icy dome,
That this rather friendly Eskimo had built as his home.
He took his place at the table, where sitting beside him,
Were a wobbly Walrus, and a p...p...perky P...Penguin.

'Pwease join us for dinner?' The huge Walrus growled,
As he twirled his moustache and wobbled his jowls.

'Oh yes p...p...please you must, we wouldn't want to be rude'
Chirped the Penguin *'Have a seat, we've got p...p...plenty of food!'*

The table was packed with what seemed to consist,
Of a full Christmas dinner, with a rather strange twist.
The turkey, the sprouts, the cranberry sauce,
The roasties, the carrots, in fact every course,
Were all made out of snow, or carved out of ice,
But don't get me wrong it still looked very nice.

'I've heard of cold turkey but this is just silly,'
Holly mumbled, now starting to feel rather chilly.
'Come on Ivan' She snapped, *'There's no time to waste.*
We've got to get going, so stop stuffing your face!

'Thanks so much,' Sighed Ivan, *'But we'll have to say no.*
It looks like we have quite a long way to go.
We have to find Archie and Poppy you see,
If we don't there'll be no presents under their tree.'

'Well that's weally wotten luck, we do wish you could stay'
Said the walrus as his huge whiskers wobbled away.
'What a terrible p...p...pickle, you p...p...poor little things!'
Piped the Penguin with a waddle and a flap of her wings.

'Then we'll help!' The friendly faced Eskimo cried,
'I think I know someone who can give you a ride.'

And with that he jumped up and pulled out a saw,
And proceeded to cut a big hole in the floor.
Before plucking out the large chunk of ice and snow,
To reveal the freezing cold water below.

Then he and his chums all started to sing,
And without any warning, dunked their heads right in.

'My goodness' Said Holly, *'What on earth's going on?*
I really must say, that is an odd song.'

Then the Eskimo popped up and said with a smile.
'We're just calling our friend, he'll be here in a while.'
But before they could question this jolly old soul,
A Killer Whale poked its snout out of the hole!

Just jump on my back,' Grinned the huge Killer Whale,
'I'll get you where you're going in two shakes of my tail.'

So the pair of rag dolls, held their breath and jumped in,
And grabbed on tightly to the huge Whale's fin.

'Good Wuck!' Said the Walrus and twiddled his tash,
And then they were off with a wave and a splash.

* * *

They swum through the ocean as the Whale's tail swished,
And they saw every kind of colourful fish.
Squids! Shellfish! Seahorses! Anchovies! Octopi!
Bottlenosed Dolphins, who smiled and swam by.
Conger eels did the conga, and Flying Fish flew,
Stingrays stung, and Blue Whales…blew?

They swam and they swam until finally they reached,
The shores of a beautiful tropical beach.

'You've still got a few hours until Christmas day'
Said the Whale, *'I wish I could take you all the way'*
'But alas this is me,' He said spying the sand,
'The truth is my tail's much slower on land.'

So they jumped off his back and on his way he went
'Thanks Mr Whale, you've been a real gent!'

* * *

'So what to do now and where to begin?'
Mused Ivan as he thoughtfully scratched his cloth chin.
When suddenly something strange caught Holly's eye,
And she saw a mischievous Monkey swing by.

'Merry Christmas,' Grinned the Monkey as he swung from a tree,
'You've arrived just in time to join us for tea.'

And he swooped down and grabbed them with a smile on his face,
Then they swung through the jungle at a lightning pace.

They zipped through the trees, going frightfully quick,
'*This is great fun,*' Said Holly, '*Though I may well be sick.*'

'*Here we are!*' Screeched the Monkey and he dropped to the floor.
'*The table's been laid but we'll add two places more!*'

He sat down at a tree stump that was laid out for lunch,
And sitting beside him were a very odd bunch.
A peculiar parrot with bright feathered wings,
And a slithery snake, coiled up like a spring.

They were licking their lips with a hungry delight,
'*My goodness,*' Said Ivan, '*That is a strange sight!*'
'*Pleassssse join ussss for sssssupper?*' Hissed the slippery snake.
'*We've got crackers,*' Squawked the parrot, '*And pieces of eight.*'

'*Yes join us, you must, we don't want to be rude,*'
Howled the Monkey '*Have a seat, we've got plenty of food!*'

'*We've got crackers,*' Squawked the parrot, '*And pieces of eight*'
He repeated, which between us was a rather strange trait.

The table was packed with what seemed to consist,
Of a full Christmas dinner, with a rather strange twist.
The turkey, the sprouts, and the cranberry sauce,
The roasties, the carrots, in fact every course,
Were all made out of bananas, or other strange fruits,
Even the sausages looked more like tree roots.

'*Now don't get me wrong, I like five a day,*'
Holly smirked '*But we really should be on our way,
We have to find Archie and Poppy you see,
If we don't there'll be no presents under their tree.*'

'Thanks so much,' Smiled Ivan *'But we'll have to say no,'*
It looks like we still have a long way to go.'

'Sssssso sssseriously sssssad,' The snake slowly exclaimed.
'What a shame,' Said the Parrot, then again, *'What a shame.'*

'Then we'll help!' The mischievous monkey cried,
'I think I know someone who can give you a ride.'
And with that he jumped up and he and his chums,
Began beating out a rhythm on their huge jungle drums.

'My goodness' Said Holly *'What on earth's happening?*
I've never heard anyone make such a din!'
'What did you say? I'm afraid I can't hear,'
Shouted Ivan, as he put his hands over his ears.

'We're calling our friend, you simply must meet her,'
And then suddenly out sprang a sleek spotty cheetah!

'Just jump on my back' Purred the big spotted cat,
'I'll get you where you're going in two seconds flat.'

'Sssseee you ssssoon,' Hissed the snake, and with that they were gone,
And as the Cheetah sped off they were sure to hold on.

They shot through the jungle with the wind in their hair,
At such wonderful speed they flew through the air.
Jumping over branches and dodging round trees,
Seeing everything the jungle had on offer to see.

Crocodiles and Cockatoos! And Tapirs and Tigers!
Elephants! And Orangutans!
And Sloths! And giant Spiders!
Tree Frogs climbed trees, And Fruit Bats were batty,
Anteaters ate ants, And Big Cats were catty!

Eventually the jungle's trees came to an end,
And the twins bade goodbye to their fast furry friend.
'I'm afraid to say this is where I must stop…
I can't run in the desert, it's simply too hot!'

* * *

So she gave them a grin and waved them goodbye,
And as the Cheetah sprang off, Ivan looked to the skies.
'It'll be Christmas morning before very soon,
And now we're stuck in a desert with nothing but sand dunes!
We've been through the snow and the whole jungle too,
But we still haven't found them, what on earth shall we do?'

'Found who?' Said a voice catching them by surprise,
And they turned to see three Camels who looked rather wise.
'It's just we're also looking for someone you see,'
Said Camel Number One, or was it Camel Number Three?
'Are you looking for Archie and Poppy too?'
Number Three shook his head, or was that Number Two?
'Archie and Poppy? No that doesn't sound right,
The person we're looking for is being born tonight!'
'Tonight!' Exclaimed Holly, *'But how will you know!?'*
'Well a star will appear showing us which way to go…'

Holly thought this sounded odd but she didn't say a word,
After all her own quest was equally absurd.

Then Camels One, Two and Three, gestured down to the sand,
Where laid out on a rug was a picnic so grand.
'In the meantime we're just settling down to some food,
You're welcome to join us, we wouldn't want to be rude.'

Holly looked over at Ivan and then rolled her eyes,
'Here we go again, well what a surprise.'

Their picnic was packed with what seemed to consist,
Of a full Christmas dinner, with a rather strange twist.
The turkey, the sprouts, the cranberry sauce,
The roasties, the carrots, in fact every course,
Were all made out of sand, yes, of sand it was made!
And instead of knives and forks they had buckets and spades.

'I prefer my turkey a little more moist,'
Whispered Holly to Ivan, whilst lowering her voice.
'Desert for dessert, doesn't sound very great,
Who'd want a whole sand castle sat on their plate?'

'Thanks so much,' Smiled Ivan, *'But we'll have to say no,'*
We still seem to have quite a long way to go.'

But then suddenly the Camels all looked to the skies,
'There it is!' Cried One with excitement in his eyes.
'It's happening, there's the star to show us the way.'
'Hang on,' Replied Ivan, *'That's no star, that's a sleigh!'*
'It's Santa!' Cried Holly, *'Hey Santa down here!'*
But old Santa was just a bit too far to hear.

'We must catch him,' Said Ivan, *'There's so much at stake,*
We have to find Archie and Poppy before they awake.
If we don't get to their stockings before very long,
Then the whole of their Christmas will go horribly wrong.'

'Then we'll help!' The curious Camel cried,
'I think I know someone who can give you a ride.'

'What a good idea,' Said Camel Number Two,
And he pursed his fat lips and he blew and he blew.
And out came the loudest whistle you ever did hear,
It was so awfully loud Holly covered her ears.

'My goodness,' She shouted, *'Now I've seen everything.*
Whistling camels, drumming monkeys and penguins who sing!'

Then far off in the sky they saw a small dot,
Which grew bigger and bigger the closer it got.

'Is it a bird, is it a plane?' An excited Ivan chimed,
'It's a bird,' Said Number Three, *'You were right the first time.'*

And before long a giant Eagle swooped into view,
And through the night sky the bird gracefully flew.
Before landing at their feet with a smile on its beak,
Then it flapped its giant wings and it started to speak.

'You whistled for me?' The great big birdy said,
'Yes we did' Said Number Two, with a nod of his head.
'These chaps need a lift, can you help with their plight?'
'Of course,' Said the bird, *'Jump on and hold tight!'*

'We must get where we're going before Christmas Day'
Shouted Ivan excited, 'Now follow that sleigh!'

Then off they flew on a wing and a prayer,
And before long they found themselves high in the air.

* * *

They looked down at the desert that zoomed past below,
Seeing everything the desert had on offer to show.
There was Sand, sand and sand! And a bit more sand too,
With the occasional cactus that popped into view,
Then... Sand, sand and sand, all topped off with more sand.
'I must say,' Muttered Holly, 'The Desert sure is bland.'

They followed Santa's sleigh as it whizzed through the
sky,
And over the horizon the sun started to rise.

'We'll never catch up he's simply too fast,'
Moaned Ivan as he watched Santa's reindeer shoot past.
But the Eagle flapped its wings with all of its might,
And they followed the sleigh through the rest of the night.

* * *

Till eventually after what seemed like forever,
And the poor Eagle's wings ached in every feather,
They looked up to see Santa parking his sled.
'He's stopping!' Cried Holly, as she pointed ahead.

They watched as Santa crawled across a rooftop,
Then zipped down a chimney with a satisfying *plop!*

Over to the roof the giant bird flew,
'Just set us down here if that's okay with you?'

And the two toys jumped off, and waved to their friend,
'You've been a great help Mr Bird thanks again.'

Then they jumped down the chimney as quick as they could,
Landing with a bump on a pile of old firewood.
At the bottom sat Santa looking awfully confused.
'I'm two presents short, now that simply won't do.
How could this have happened? I really don't know,
What on earth will I do? Oh No ho ho ho…'

Then out popped Holly and Ivan both covered in soot,
And as black as the night from the head to the foot.

'I'm so sorry Santa that we're in such a state,
But we got rather lost, I hope that we're not too late.
We had tea with a Walrus and rode on a Whale,
Caught a lift with a Monkey who swung from its tail.
Saw a Parrot who weirdly said everything twice,
Then spent time with three Camels who were all very nice,
Then finally an Eagle took us the rest of the way,
…And we ended up here by following your sleigh!'

Santa stared at the toys looking rather confused,
Then burst into a laugh, as if thoroughly amused.
'You wonderful toys, you're here just in time!'
And the clock in the corner then started to chime.

'Now dust yourselves off and get under the tree!'
He chuckled as his huge belly wobbled with glee.
'Well what an adventure, you're both so very clever,
I'm sure Archie and Poppy will have the best Christmas ever!'

Then he tucked them both in their stockings and waved them goodbye,
And with a final '*Ho ho ho*' and a wink of his eye,
He zipped back up the chimney and onto his sled.
And they heard the faint tinkle of sleigh bells overhead.

Holly looked to Ivan and gave him a smile,
'I told you we'd make it, I knew all the while.
But when I woke up this morning I would not have believed,
That we'd have such an eventful Christmas Eve!'

And with that their eyes closed and they drifted to sleep,
As the Christmas morn' robin soon started to cheep.
Whilst up above in a bedroom a sister and brother,
Stirred from their sleep and turned to each other,
Then with a tremble in her voice the little girl did say…

'Archie wake up, it's Christmas Day!'

THE PLAY

Holly and Ivan's Christmas Adventure by Oliver Lansley was first performed at the Lyric Hammersmith on December 1st 2011.

Co-produced by Pins and Needles Productions and the Lyric Hammersmith.

Original cast:

Rob Cavazos: Storyteller 2, Ivan, Walrus, Parrot, Camel

Katie Elin-Salt: Storyteller 3, Holly, Penguin, Snake, Camel

Dan Gingell: Storyteller 1, Santa, Eskimo, Killer Whale, Monkey, Cheetah, Camel, Eagle

Writer: Oliver Lansley

Adapted for the stage by Oliver Lansley and Emma Earle

Director: Emma Earle

Design: Zoe Squire

Lighting Design: George Ogilvie

Composer: Tom Elstob

Production Assistant: Lee Rayner

Costume Maker: Robyn Manton

Artwork created by Zoe Squire

Pins and Needles Productions is committed to creating inspiring visual theatre that unites both physical and text-based work. We are interested in telling highly theatrical stories for young and old, and enjoy making work that celebrates the power of the imagination, never forgetting the role the audience plays in the live event. The company was established in 2009 by Director/Designer partnership Emma Earle and Zoe Squire.

www.pinsandneedlesproductions.co.uk

The Lyric Hammersmith is one of the UK's leading producing theatres. For over 100 years we have created some of the country's most groundbreaking and celebrated theatrical work. We have also gained a national reputation for our work with and for children and young people.

Find us at www.lyric.co.uk

With special thanks to the Earles, the Squires, Dominic Oliver Kelly, Madeleine Hunter, Jacob Fisher, Jessica Maliphant and everyone else who helped to make this production happen.

Emma would like to dedicate this production to her little brother Rowan.

A moonlit landscape in the snow. A snow globe hangs from a magical tree. From within the tree emerge three snowy STORYTELLERS. Music plays and the snow globe starts to glow. The STORYTELLERS pluck the snow globe from the tree. There is a crank handle on the side like an old music box. The STORYTELLERS turn the handle and a warm voice begins...

V.O: Holly and Ivan were two little twins,
They wore the same clothes and they said the same things.
But Holly and Ivan were different from most,
Which probably sounds like a ridiculous boast.
As each boy and girl is unique, in their own special way.

STORYTELLER ONE: Like Sarah Spondel from Scagglethorpe shall we say…

STORYTELLER TWO: Whose nose curves up so much at the end That skiers might wish to jump from the bend.

We see a brief glimpse of Sarah Spondel.

STORYTELLER THREE: Or Billy Birthwhistle from Bognor who's quite a strange sight,
As his left ear is a good deal smaller than his right.

And now it's the turn of Billy Birthwhistle.

STORYTELLER ONE: Which makes it look slightly further away,
Making Billy appear to always face the wrong way.

V.O: But Holly and Ivan differed from most girls and boys.
Because Holly and Ivan were actually...

STORYTELLER TWO/STORYTELLER THREE /STORYTELLER ONE: Toys!

Out of nowhere, two rag dolls appear.

V.O.: Rag dolls to be precise, with button eyes and woollen hair,
Stitched up and sewn with a great deal of care.
They were born in Santa's grotto far far far away,

STORYTELLER TWO: Where it's so cold, that sometimes even the words that you say

STORYTELLER ONE: Will freeze the instant they're spoken aloud

The STORYTELLER takes a deep breath and, like a child blowing bubbles, a 'Happy Christmas' paper chain is blown from their mouth.

STORYTELLER THREE: Meaning sentences as well as snow need to get ploughed.

V.O.: They were made by elves, a peculiar race,

STORYTELLER TWO: Who are pointy of ear,

STORYTELLER THREE: And rosy of face!

We see a glimpse of an elf.

V.O.: Now Elves don't receive money for the toys that they make
Instead they are given their payment in cake.

STORYTELLER THREE: Fairy cakes to be precise as they don't eat much else,

STORYTELLER TWO: Which to be honest I'm not sure is good for their health.

STORYTELLER THREE: Bacon fairy cakes for breakfast, or fried egg ones for brunch,

STORYTELLER TWO: Then cheese and cucumber fairy cakes will follow for lunch.

STORYTELLER ONE: And some sausage and chips fairy cakes for supper and tea,

STORYTELLER THREE: With a nice fairy cake for pudding, if they're still hungry.

V.O: Now our story starts on that one special night,
That fills every new toy with a sense of delight.

STORYTELLER TWO: Monday?

V.O: I hear one Simple Simon suggest…

STORYTELLER THREE: No not Monday, you fool, Mondays aren't the best.

STORYTELLER ONE: Easter perhaps?

STORYTELLER TWO: Or Bonfire night?

V.O.: Well they're both indeed fun but they're still not right.

STORYTELLER THREE: It's Christmas Eve of course!

V.O.: That one day of the year, that fills every new toy with a sense of good cheer.

STORYTELLER THREE: Because it's the day that they meet their new families.

V.O: All those little boys and girls who've been doing good deeds.

STORYTELLER TWO: Like helping old ladies to put on their hats,

We see an old lady being assisted in putting her hat on in the mirror.

STORYTELLER ONE: And knitting woollen jackets for bald dogs and cats.

And now we see a frenzy of knitting hands create mini jackets for animals.

V.O.: And so we begin on that bestest of days
    With Santa starting to fill up his sleigh...

* * *

Music plays, transporting us to SANTA's grotto, far far away. The STORYTELLERS control a rod of marionette toys, while HOLLY and IVAN wait patiently at the back.

STORYTELLER TWO: The toys jostled for a place at the front of the queue.

SANTA: *'Don't worry,'*

STORYTELLER THREE: Said Santa,

SANTA: *'There's room for all of you...*

STORYTELLER TWO: Then he pulled open his sack and said,

SANTA: *'In you go...'*

STORYTELLER TWO: And followed this up with a mighty,

SANTA: *'Ho Ho Ho...'*

STORYTELLER THREE: Santa had a strange habit of ho ho ho-ing when he spoke,
    Even if what he'd said wasn't really a joke.
    Now it was usually fine, him being always amused
    But it became a bit awkward if he was given bad news.

SANTA: *'I'm sorry to hear your frog died ho ho ho...*
    What do you mean I sound happy? I'm sad don't you know ho ho ho ho ho ho ho ho...'

STORYTELLER TWO: As the queue of toys started to jump in the sack,
    Poor Holly and Ivan were stuck at the back.

STORYTELLER THREE: And soon the sack was so full, right up to the brim,

That Holly and Ivan almost didn't fit in.

STORYTELLER TWO: Then all of a sudden Santa yelled,

SANTA: '*Go! Ho ho…*'

STORYTELLER TWO: And the reindeers reared up and sped off through the snow.

Music. SANTA's sleigh takes off, led by two ukulele playing reindeer on reins. They veer this way and that, avoiding oncoming obstacles and braving inclement weather. The dolls hold onto the sleigh for dear life.

STORYTELLER ONE: Holly and Ivan held on as tight as they could,

But as the sleigh's speed got faster it was simply no good,

STORYTELLER THREE: Their raggy doll fingers just couldn't hold on,

STORYTELLER TWO: And with a big gust of wind, that was it, they were gone.

HOLLY and IVAN fly through the air before falling in slow motion through snowflakes and wind.

STORYTELLER ONE: They tumbled through the air to the earth far below,

And were lucky to land in a big pile of snow.

A miniature SANTA and his reindeer fly across the giant moon in silhouette. HOLLY and IVAN are now human sized but they continue to carry their dolls with them, everywhere they go.

HOLLY: *'Where are we?'*

STORYTELLER ONE: Moaned Holly, as she rubbed her bruised bum.

HOLLY: *'I must say that falling really isn't much fun.'*

STORYTELLER ONE: Ivan got to his feet and looked all around,

Suddenly feeling much more lost than found.

IVAN: *'I think that we're nowhere, and this is the middle,*
But what we do next? Well that's really a riddle'

A magical sound. HOLLY and IVAN pull out large gift tags on strings from their clothes.

STORYTELLER ONE: Then suddenly they spotted, a most peculiar thing,

Two tags of brown paper, both tied on with string.

And on each tag were names, of a young girl and boy,

HOLLY: *'They must be our owners!'*

STORYTELLER ONE: Squealed Holly with joy.

IVAN: *'Archie and Poppy,'*

STORYTELLER ONE: Read Ivan with care,

IVAN: *'Well I must say they sound like a most pleasant pair'.*

HOLLY: *'We must find them!'*

STORYTELLER ONE: Said Holly,

HOLLY: *'Whatever it takes!*
They can't wake up without presents, for Christmas sakes!'

* * *

The snow globe glows once again.

STORYTELLER ONE: But how will they find them?

STORYTELLER TWO: And where will they go?

STORYTELLER THREE: And when will they get there, I simply must know!

STORYTELLER ONE: Can they really succeed in their Christmassy quest?

V.O.: Well if you stop asking questions then I'll tell you the rest...

Music.

V.O.: The pair walked for hours through the freezing cold snow,
Neither of them knowing which way they should go.
They shivered with cold as the wind rushed around,
And fresh snowflakes fell fast and covered the ground.

It snows on HOLLY and IVAN. They make their way through the snow, cold and afraid. Then HOLLY throws a snowball at IVAN and a giggly snowball fight ensues.

V.O.: Until finally through the blizzard a furry figure drew near...

A giant, dark figure is silhouetted against the moon.

IVAN: *'It's the abominable snowman!'*

V.O.: Cried Ivan in fear.
Then he hid behind Holly, but out of the snow,
Instead of a monster came a smiley Eskimo...

* * *

HOLLY: *'I knew it wasn't a monster,'*

STORYTELLER THREE: Said Holly, shaking her head,

IVAN: *'So did I...'*

STORYTELLER TWO: Replied Ivan, though his face went quite red.

HOLLY *uses her doll as a protective shield.*

HOLLY: *'So sorry to trouble you, but are you Archie or Poppy?'*

STORYTELLER TWO: The Eskimo looked down at this strange talking dolly.

ESKIMO: *'I'm Sorry,'*

STORYTELLER TWO: He said,

ESKIMO: *'I don't know who they are…'*

STORYTELLER TWO: Then leaned in with a smile and did something bizarre.

He bent down and rubbed his red nose against theirs,

The *ESKIMO* kisses the doll.

STORYTELLER THREE: Poor Holly was really caught quite unawares.

IVAN: *'Don't worry,'*

STORYTELLER TWO: Whispered Ivan,

IVAN: *'That's how they say Hi,'*

STORYTELLER THREE: But she was too busy blushing to give a reply.

ESKIMO: *'So lovely to meet you,'*

STORYTELLER TWO: The Eskimo cried,

ESKIMO: *'We're about to have dinner, so come on inside!'*

The *ESKIMO* pulls a miniature igloo from his pocket and places it on the palm of his hand, in front of the two dolls. It is lit from within, and gently illuminates their faces.

STORYTELLER THREE: Then through the snowfall they spotted a light,

And a house built of ice cubes emerged from the night.

IVAN: *'It's an igloo!'*

STORYTELLER ONE: Cried Ivan,

HOLLY: *'An ig-who?'*

STORYTELLER ONE: Replied Holly,

HOLLY: *'It looks like a super-sized tortoise ice lolly!'*

IVAN: *'Don't be so silly, there's people inside.'*

STORYTELLER ONE: Ivan said with a sigh and a roll of his eyes.

And poking out from the roof they could clearly see,

The top of a colourful Christmas tree.

Music. The trio pass behind the magical tree and reappear on the other side. The space is now an igloo.

STORYTELLER TWO: And so in they walked to the big icy dome,

STORYTELLER THREE: That this rather friendly Eskimo had built as his home.

STORYTELLER ONE: He took his place at the table, where sitting beside him,

STORYTELLER 2 takes out a WALRUS headdress from a box and places it on their head.

WALRUS: Were a wobbly Walrus,

STORYTELLER 3 takes out a PENGUIN headdress from a box and places it on their head.

PENGUIN: And a p...p...perky P...Penguin.

WALRUS: *'Pwease join us for dinner?'*

STORYTELLER ONE: The huge Walrus growled,

WALRUS: As he twirled his moustache and wobbled his jowls.

PENGUIN: *'Oh yes p...p...please you must, we wouldn't want to be rude,'*

STORYTELLER ONE: Chirped the Penguin

PENGUIN: *'Have a seat, we've got p...p...plenty of food!'*

Music. The below song is sung to ukulele music in the style of a barbershop quartet.

ALL: The table was packed with what seemed to consist,
Of a full Christmas dinner, with a rather strange twist.
The turkey, the sprouts, the cranberry sauce,
The roasties, the carrots, in fact every course,
Were all made out of snow, or carved out of ice,
But don't get me wrong it still looked very nice.

The song ends with a rhythmic section made up of the noises of eating Christmas dinner.

* * *

HOLLY: *'I've heard of cold turkey but this is just silly,'*

STORYTELLER ONE: Holly mumbled, now starting to feel rather chilly.

HOLLY: *'Come on Ivan,'*

STORYTELLER ONE: She snapped,

HOLLY: *'There's no time to waste.
We've got to get going, so stop stuffing your face!*

IVAN: *'Thanks so much,'*

STORYTELLER ONE: Sighed Ivan,

IVAN: *'But we'll have to say no.*
It looks like we have quite a long way to go.'

HOLLY: *'We have to find Archie and Poppy you see,*
If we don't there'll be no presents under their tree.'

WALRUS: *'Well that's weally wotten luck, we do wish you could*
stay,'

STORYTELLER ONE: Said the walrus as his huge whiskers
wobbled away.

PENGUIN: *'What a terrible p...p...pickle, you p...p...poor little*
things!'

STORYTELLER TWO: Piped the Penguin with a waddle and a
flap of her wings.

ESKIMO: *'Then we'll help!'*

STORYTELLER TWO: The friendly faced Eskimo cried,

ESKIMO: *'I think I know someone who can give you a ride.'*

STORYTELLER TWO: And with that he jumped up and
pulled out a saw,
And proceeded to cut a big hole in the floor.

We see and hear the ESKIMO cutting a hole in the ice. The
ice pops out like a cork out of a bottle.

STORYTELLER THREE: Before plucking out the large chunk
of ice and snow,
To reveal the freezing cold water below.

STORYTELLER TWO: Then he and his chums all started to
sing,

The trio form a barbershop quartet tableau and harmonise.

STORYTELLER ONE: And without any warning, dunked their heads right in.

The trio turn up stage and dunk their heads in the hole. We hear warbled, underwater singing including mangled versions of Christmas songs.

HOLLY: *'My goodness,'*

STORYTELLER TWO: Said Holly,

HOLLY: *'What on earth's going on?*
I really must say, that is an odd song.'

STORYTELLER TWO: Then the Eskimo popped up and said with a smile,

ESKIMO: *'We're just calling our friend, he'll be here in a while.'*

The ESKIMO jumps into the hole.

STORYTELLER TWO: But before they could question this jolly old soul,

STORYTELLER THREE: A Killer Whale poked its snout out of the hole!

The STORYTELLER reappears with a large whale head puppet. It breaches out of the hole, blowing water from its snout.

KILLER WHALE: *'Just jump on my back,'*

STORYTELLER TWO: Grinned the huge Killer Whale,

KILLER WHALE: *'I'll get you where you're going in two shakes of my tail,'*

The STORYTELLERS jump in the hole with the whale. The HOLLY and IVAN dolls ride on the whale's head, bobbing on the waves.

STORYTELLER TWO and STORYTELLER THREE: So the pair of rag dolls, held their breath and jumped in,
And grabbed on tightly to the huge Whale's fin.

WALRUS: *'Good Wuck!'*

STORYTELLER ONE: Said the Walrus and twiddled his tash,

STORYTELLER THREE: And then they were off with a wave and a splash.

The whale head disappears into the hole after a final spurt of water.

* * *

Music. Lights change. Bubbles. We are in a beautiful, underwater world. The STORYTELLERS appear wearing vintage swimwear. We see a synchronised movement sequence where the STORYTELLERS create a range of sea creatures, from crabs to jelly fish, mermaids to shoals of fish. We see a miniature version of HOLLY and IVAN riding the whale.

STORYTELLER ONE: They swum through the ocean as the Whale's tail swished,
And they saw every kind of colourful fish.

STORYTELLER THREE: Squids!

STORYTELLER TWO: Shellfish!

STORYTELLER THREE: Seahorses!

STORYTELLER TWO: Anchovies!

STORYTELLER THREE: Octopi!

STORYTELLER TWO: Bottlenosed Dolphins, who smiled and swam by.

STORYTELLER THREE: Conger eels did the conga,

STORYTELLER TWO: And Flying Fish flew,

STORYTELLER THREE: Stingrays stung,

STORYTELLER TWO: And Blue Whales... blew?

STORYTELLER THREE: They swam and they swam until finally they reached,
The shores of a beautiful tropical beach.

Music ends with a great splash as the whale head re-emerges from the hole with the dolls, on the shores of a tropical beach. Lights change.

* * *

KILLER WHALE: *'You've still got a few hours until Christmas day,'*

STORYTELLER TWO: Said the Whale,

KILLER WHALE: *'I wish I could take you all the way.'*
'But alas this is me,'

STORYTELLER TWO: He said spying the sand,

KILLER WHALE: *'The truth is my tail's much slower on land.'*

STORYTELLER THREE: So they jumped off his back and on his way he went,

IVAN/HOLLY: *'Thanks Mr Whale, you've been a real gent!'*

The whale head disappears.

* * *

IVAN: *'So what to do now and where to begin?'*

STORYTELLER THREE: Mused Ivan as he thoughtfully
   scratched his cloth chin.

STORYTELLER TWO: When suddenly something strange
   caught Holly's eye,
   And she saw a mischievous Monkey swing by.

MONKEY: *'Merry Christmas,'*

STORYTELLER TWO: Grinned the Monkey as he swung
   from a tree,

MONKEY: *'You've arrived just in time to join us for tea'.*

**Music. Vines of colourful Chinese lanterns drop from
the sky. The MONKEY takes HOLLY and IVAN's hands and
swings onto a vine.**

STORYTELLER TWO: And he swooped down and grabbed
   them with a smile on his face,
   Then they swung through the jungle at a lightning pace.

**The MONKEY swings through the trees with HOLLY and IVAN,
from vine to vine. IVAN gets stuck. HOLLY is enjoying herself.**

STORYTELLER ONE: They zipped through the trees, going
   frightfully quick,

HOLLY: *'This is great fun,'*

STORYTELLER TWO: Said Holly,

HOLLY: *'Though I may well be sick.'*

They all dance. The music ends.

* * *

MONKEY: *'Here we are!'*

STORYTELLER TWO: Screeched the Monkey and he
   dropped to the floor.

MONKEY: *'The table's been laid but we'll add two places more!'*

STORYTELLER THREE: He sat down at a tree stump that was laid out for lunch,

And sitting beside him were a very odd bunch.

STORYTELLER 2 takes a PARROT headdress from a box and places it on their head.

STORYTELLER TWO: A peculiar parrot with bright feathered wings,

STORYTELLER 3 takes a SNAKE headdress from a box and places it on their head.

STORYTELLER THREE: And a slithery snake, coiled up like a spring.

STORYTELLER ONE: They were licking their lips with a hungry delight,

IVAN: *'My goodness,'*

STORYTELLER ONE: Said Ivan,

IVAN: *'that is a strange sight!'*

SNAKE: *'Pleassssse join ussss for ssssssuper?'*

STORYTELLER ONE: Hissed the slippery snake.

PARROT: *'We've got crackers,'*

STORYTELLER ONE: Squawked the parrot,

PARROT: *'And pieces of eight.'*

MONKEY: *'Yes join us, you must, we don't want to be rude,'*

STORYTELLER THREE: Howled the Monkey.

MONKEY: *'Have a seat, we've got plenty of food!'*

PARROT: *'We've got crackers,'*

STORYTELLER THREE: Squawked the parrot,

PARROT: *'And pieces of eight,'*

STORYTELLER THREE: He repeated, which between us was a rather strange trait.

Music. Party time. Animal calls and sounds of the carnival.

ALL: The table was packed with what seemed to consist,
Of a full Christmas dinner, with a rather strange twist.
The turkey, the sprouts, and the cranberry sauce,
The roasties, the carrots, in fact every course,
Were all made out of bananas, or other strange fruits,
Even the sausages looked more like tree roots.

The song turns into a rhythmic section involving messy eating noises.

* * *

HOLLY: *'Now don't get me wrong, I like five a day,'*

STORYTELLER ONE: Holly smirked,

HOLLY: *'But we really should be on our way,*
We have to find Archie and Poppy you see,
If we don't there'll be no presents under their tree'

IVAN: *'Thanks so much,'*

STORYTELLER ONE: Smiled Ivan,

IVAN: *'But we'll have to say no'*
It looks like we still have a long way to go.'

SNAKE: *'Ssssssso sssseriously sssssad,'*

STORYTELLER ONE: The snake slowly exclaimed.

PARROT: *'What a shame,'*

STORYTELLER ONE: Said the Parrot, then again,

PARROT: *'What a shame,'*

MONKEY: *'Then we'll help!'*

STORYTELLER TWO: The mischievous monkey cried,

MONKEY: *'I think I know someone who can give you a ride.'*

STORYTELLER THREE: And with that he jumped up and he and his chums,
Began beating out a rhythm on their huge jungle drums.

The trio start playing a raucous jungle rhythm on drums and other percussion instruments.

* * *

HOLLY: *'My goodness,'*

STORYTELLER TWO: Said Holly,

HOLLY: *'What on earth's happening?*
I've never heard anyone make such a din!'

IVAN: *'What did you say? I'm afraid I can't hear,'*

STORYTELLER THREE: Shouted Ivan, as he put his hands over his ears.

MONKEY: *'We're calling our friend, you simply must meet her,'*

STORYTELLER THREE: And then suddenly out sprang a sleek spotty cheetah!

Big drum solo finish followed by the arrival of the CHEETAH puppet head.

* * *

CHEETAH: *Just jump on my back,'*

STORYTELLER TWO: Purred the big spotted cat,

CHEETAH: *'I'll get you where you're going in two seconds flat.'*

The HOLLY and IVAN dolls are fixed onto the CHEETAH's head.

SNAKE: *'Ssssseee you sssssoon,'*

STORYTELLER TWO: Hissed the snake, and with that they were gone,

And as the Cheetah sped off they were sure to hold on.

Music. HOLLY and IVAN ride the jungle roller coaster. It's a bumpy ride.

STORYTELLER THREE: They shot through the jungle with the wind in their hair,

At such wonderful speed they flew through the air.

STORYTELLER ONE: Jumping over branches and dodging round trees,

Seeing everything the jungle had on offer to see.

Music changes. They then find themselves in a canoe on a night safari, paddling and spotting animals through binoculars.

STORYTELLER TWO: Crocodiles and Cockatoos!

STORYTELLER THREE: And Tapirs and Tigers!

STORYTELLER TWO: Elephants!

STORYTELLER THREE: And Orangutans!

STORYTELLER TWO: And Sloths!

STORYTELLER THREE: And giant Spiders!

STORYTELLER TWO: Tree Frogs climbed trees,

STORYTELLER THREE: And Fruit Bats were batty,

STORYTELLER TWO: Anteaters ate ants,

STORYTELLER THREE: And Big Cats were catty!

Music ends.

STORYTELLER TWO: Eventually the jungle's trees came to an end,
And the twins bade goodbye to their fast furry friend.

CHEETAH: *'I'm afraid to say this is where I must stop…*
I can't run in the desert, it's simply too hot!'

***HOLLY* and *IVAN* dismount. The *CHEETAH* disappears. Lights change. It is night in the desert.**

* * *

STORYTELLER THREE: So she gave them a grin and waved them goodbye,
And as the Cheetah sprang off, Ivan looked to the skies.

IVAN: *'It'll be Christmas morning before very soon,*
And now we're stuck in a desert with nothing but sand dunes!
We've been through the snow and the whole jungle too,
But we still haven't found them, what on earth shall we do?'

* * *

Triplet camel heads appear. They wear sunglasses and sashay like Motown backing singers.

CAMEL 1 (STORYTELLER ONE): *'Found who?'*

STORYTELLER TWO: Said a voice catching them by surprise,

STORYTELLER THREE: And they turned to see three Camels who looked rather wise.

CAMEL 1 (STORYTELLER ONE): *'It's just we're also looking for someone you see,'*

STORYTELLER THREE: Said Camel Number One,

STORYTELLER TWO: Or was it Camel Number Three?

IVAN: *'Are you looking for Archie and Poppy too?'*

STORYTELLER THREE: Number Three shook his head,

STORYTELLER TWO: Or was that Number Two?

CAMEL 3 (STORYTELLER ONE): *'Archie and Poppy? No that doesn't sound right,*
The person we're looking for is being born tonight!'

HOLLY: *'Tonight!'*

STORYTELLER TWO: Exclaimed Holly,

HOLLY: *'But how will you know!?'*

CAMEL 2 (STORYTELLER ONE): *'Well a star will appear showing us which way to go…'*

STORYTELLER THREE: Holly thought this sounded odd but she didn't say a word,
After all her own quest was equally absurd.

STORYTELLER TWO: Then Camels One, Two and Three, gestured down to the sand,
Where laid out on a rug was a picnic so grand.

CAMEL 1 (STORYTELLER ONE): *'In the meantime we're just settling down to some food,*
You're welcome to join us, we wouldn't want to be rude.'

STORYTELLER THREE: Holly looked over at Ivan and then rolled her eyes,

HOLLY: *'Here we go again, well what a surprise.'*

Music. The Camels sing in a Motown style, performing slides and finger clicks while bathed in the light of a starry mirror ball.

ALL: Their picnic was packed with what seemed to consist,
Of a full Christmas dinner, with a rather strange twist.
The turkey, the sprouts, the cranberry sauce,
The roasties, the carrots, in fact every course,
Were all made out of sand, yes, of sand it was made!
And instead of knives and forks they had buckets and spades.

A rhythmic chewing and munching section follows.

* * *

HOLLY: *'I prefer my turkey a little more moist,'*

STORYTELLER ONE: Whispered Holly to Ivan, whilst lowering her voice.

HOLLY: *'Desert for dessert, doesn't sound very great,*
Who'd want a whole sand castle sat on their plate?'

IVAN: *'Thanks so much,'*

STORYTELLER ONE: Smiled Ivan,

IVAN: *'But we'll have to say no,'*
We still seem to have quite a long way to go.'

STORYTELLER THREE: But then suddenly the Camels all looked to the skies,

CAMEL 1 (STORYTELLER ONE): *'There it is!'*

STORYTELLER THREE: Cried One with excitement in his eyes.

CAMEL 1 (STORYTELLER ONE): *'It's happening, there's the star to show us the way,'*

IVAN: *'Hang on,'*

STORYTELLER THREE: Replied Ivan,

IVAN: *'That's no star, that's a sleigh!'*

HOLLY: *'It's Santa!'*

STORYTELLER ONE: Cried Holly,

HOLLY: *'Hey Santa down here!'*

STORYTELLER ONE: But old Santa was just a bit too far to hear.

IVAN: *'We must catch him,'*

STORYTELLER ONE: Said Ivan,

IVAN: *'There's so much at stake,*
We have to find Archie and Poppy before they awake.
If we don't get to their stockings before very long,
Then the whole of their Christmas will go horribly wrong.'

CAMEL 1 (STORYTELLER ONE): *'Then we'll help!'*

STORYTELLER TWO: The curious Camel cried,

CAMEL 1 (STORYTELLER ONE): *'I think I know someone who can give you a ride,'*

CAMEL 2 (STORYTELLER ONE): *'What a good idea,'*

STORYTELLER THREE: Said Camel Number Two,
And he pursed his fat lips and he blew and he blew.

A deafening bassy whistle.

STORYTELLER TWO: And out came the loudest whistle you ever did hear,

It was so awfully loud Holly covered her ears.

HOLLY: *'My goodness,'*

STORYTELLER TWO: She shouted,

HOLLY: *'Now I've seen everything.*
Whistling camels, drumming monkeys and penguins who sing!'

STORYTELLER 1 hands over the triplet camel heads to STORYTELLERS 2 and 3.

* * *

STORYTELLER ONE: Then far off in the sky they saw a small dot,

Which grew bigger and bigger the closer it got.

IVAN: *'Is it a bird, is it a plane?'*

STORYTELLER TWO: An excited Ivan chimed,

CAMEL 3 (STORYTELLER THREE): *'It's a bird,'*

STORYTELLER TWO: Said Number Three,

CAMEL 3 (STORYTELLER THREE): *'You were right the first time.'*

A Biggles-style Eagle begins pre-flight checks at the rear of the auditorium, preparing to swoop down the aisle, through the audience.

STORYTELLER THREE: And before long a giant eagle swooped into view,

And through the night sky the bird gracefully flew.

STORYTELLER TWO: Before landing at their feet with a smile on its beak,

STORYTELLER THREE: Then it flapped its giant wings and it started to speak.

The EAGLE has landed.

EAGLE: _'You whistled for me?'_

STORYTELLER THREE: The great big birdy said,

CAMEL 2 (STORYTELLER TWO): _'Yes we did,'_

STORYTELLER TWO: Said Number Two, with a nod of his head.

CAMEL 2 (STORYTELLER TWO): _'These cats need a lift, can you help with their plight?'_

EAGLE: _'Of course,'_

STORYTELLER THREE: Said the bird,

EAGLE: _'Jump on and hold tight!'_

The HOLLY and IVAN dolls jump on, one on each wing. The EAGLE prepares for take off.

IVAN: _'We must get where we're going before Christmas Day,'_

STORYTELLER THREE: Shouted Ivan excited,

IVAN: _'Now follow that sleigh!'_

STORYTELLER THREE: Then off they flew on a wing and a prayer,
And before long they found themselves high in the air.

* * *

Music. The chase is on...

STORYTELLER TWO: They looked down at the desert that zoomed past below,
Seeing everything the desert had on offer to show.

The EAGLE makes a pilot's announcement.

EAGLE: There was

STORYTELLER THREE: Sand!

STORYTELLER TWO: Sand!

STORYTELLER THREE: And sand!

EAGLE: *'And a bit more sand too,*
With the occasional cactus that popped into view,
Then...

STORYTELLER TWO: *Sand!*

STORYTELLER THREE: *Sand!*

EAGLE: *And sand, all topped off with more sand.'*

HOLLY: *'I must say,'*

STORYTELLER TWO: Muttered Holly,

HOLLY: *'The Desert sure is bland.'*

STORYTELLER ONE: They followed Santa's sleigh as it
whizzed through the sky,
And over the horizon the sun started to rise.

We cross cut to SANTA and his reindeer cruising through
the sky singing Chirstmas songs, blissfully unaware of the
EAGLE and dolls in hot pursuit.

* * *

IVAN: *'We'll never catch up he's simply too fast,'*

STORYTELLER THREE: Moaned Ivan as he watched Santa's
reindeer shoot past.

STORYTELLER ONE: But the Eagle flapped its wings with all of its might,

And they followed the sleigh through the rest of the night.

The chase intensifies. We cut back and forth between SANTA's sleigh and the EAGLE. The EAGLE is starting to show signs of fatigue.

STORYTELLER TWO: Till eventually after what seemed like forever,

And the poor Eagle's wings ached in every feather,

They looked up to see Santa parking his sled.

HOLLY: *'He's stopping!'*

STORYTELLER TWO: Cried Holly, as she pointed ahead.

STORYTELLER ONE: They watched as Santa crawled across a rooftop,

Then zipped down a chimney with a satisfying *plop!*

We hear the sound of SANTA squeezing down a chimney and watch the EAGLE swoop towards the rooftop.

STORYTELLER THREE: Over to the roof the giant bird flew,

HOLLY/IVAN: *'Just set us down here if that's okay with you?'*

The EAGLE lands and the toys dismount.

STORYTELLER ONE: And the two toys jumped off, and waved to their friend,

HOLLY/IVAN: *'You've been a great help Mr Bird thanks again.'*

* * *

STORYTELLER THREE: Then they jumped down the chimney as quick as they could,

Landing with a bump on a pile of old firewood.

HOLLY and IVAN jump in the chimney holding hands.

Lights change. We are in a cosy sitting room.

STORYTELLER TWO: At the bottom sat Santa looking awfully confused.

SANTA: *'I'm two presents short, now that simply won't do.*
How could this have happened? I really don't know,
What on earth will I do? Oh No ho ho ho…'

STORYTELLER TWO: Then out popped Holly and Ivan both covered in soot,

And as black as the night from the head to the foot.

HOLLY and IVAN tumble out of the fireplace and land at SANTA's feet.

HOLLY: *'I'm so sorry Santa that we're in such a state,*
But we got rather lost, I hope that we're not too late.
We had tea with a Walrus and rode on a Whale,
Caught a lift with a Monkey who swung from its tail.
Saw a Parrot who weirdly said everything twice,
Then spent time with three Camels who were all very nice,
Then finally an Eagle took us the rest of the way,

IVAN: *…And we ended up here by following your sleigh!'*

STORYTELLER THREE: Santa stared at the toys looking rather confused,

Then burst into a laugh, as if thoroughly amused.

SANTA: *'You wonderful toys, you're here just in time!'*

STORYTELLER TWO: And the clock in the corner then started to chime.

The clock chimes.

SANTA: *'Now dust yourselves off and get under the tree!'*

STORYTELLER THREE: He chuckled as his huge belly wobbled
with glee.

SANTA: *'Well what an adventure, you're both so very clever,*
I'm sure Archie and Poppy will have the best Christmas ever!'

SANTA pulls out two Christmas stockings for HOLLY and IVAN.

STORYTELLER TWO: Then he tucked them both in their
stockings and waved them goodbye,
And with a final

SANTA: '*Ho ho ho*'

STORYTELLER TWO: And a wink of his eye,

STORYTELLER THREE: He zipped back up the chimney and
onto his sled.

STORYTELLER ONE: And they heard the faint tinkle of sleigh
bells overhead.

The miniature of SANTA and his reindeer sweeps across the
moon in silhouette accompanied by the sound of bells.

* * *

Music.

STORYTELLER TWO: Holly looked to Ivan and gave him a smile,

HOLLY: *'I told you we'd make it, I knew all the while.*
But when I woke up this morning I would not have believed,
That we'd have such an eventful Christmas Eve!'

The snow globe is back on the tree and begins to glow once more.

* * *

Lights change. We see ARCHIE and POPPY asleep on Christmas morning. POPPY soon starts to stir.

V.O.: And with that their eyes closed and they drifted to sleep,
As the Christmas morn' robin soon started to cheep.
Whilst up above in a bedroom a sister and brother,
Stirred from their sleep and turned to each other,
Then with a tremble in her voice the little girl did say,

Music ends.

STORYTELLER THREE: *'Archie wake up, it's Christmas Day!'*

The snow globe glows.

Lights fade.